THIS
JOURNAL
BELONGS TO:

DATE:

TRIP DETAILS

TRIP TO:

DATES FROM: / /   TO: / /

WEATHER: _____

Overall score/rating: ① ② ③ ④ ⑤ ⑥ ⑦ ⑧ ⑨ ⑩

Where we stayed:

Places we visited:

What we enjoyed most:

Favorite place(s) to eat/drink:

Places to remember next time:

NOTES & SKETCHES

TRIP DETAILS

TRIP TO:

DATES FROM: / / TO: / /

WEATHER: _____

Overall score/rating: ① ② ③ ④ ⑤ ⑥ ⑦ ⑧ ⑨ ⑩

Where we stayed:
_____

Places we visited:
_____
_____
_____

What we enjoyed most:
_____
_____

Favorite place(s) to eat/drink:
_____
_____
_____

Places to remember next time:
_____
_____

NOTES & SKETCHES

TRIP DETAILS

TRIP TO:

DATES FROM: / /   TO: / /

WEATHER:

Overall score/rating: ① ② ③ ④ ⑤ ⑥ ⑦ ⑧ ⑨ ⑩

Where we stayed:

Places we visited:

What we enjoyed most:

Favorite place(s) to eat/drink:

Places to remember next time:

NOTES & SKETCHES

TRIP DETAILS

TRIP TO:

DATES FROM: /   /   TO: /   /

WEATHER: _____

Overall score/rating: ① ② ③ ④ ⑤ ⑥ ⑦ ⑧ ⑨ ⑩

Where we stayed:

Places we visited:

What we enjoyed most:

Favorite place(s) to eat/drink:

Places to remember next time:

NOTES & SKETCHES

TRIP DETAILS

TRIP TO:

DATES FROM: / /   TO: / /

WEATHER:

Overall score/rating: ① ② ③ ④ ⑤ ⑥ ⑦ ⑧ ⑨ ⑩

Where we stayed:

Places we visited:

What we enjoyed most:

Favorite place(s) to eat/drink:

Places to remember next time:

NOTES & SKETCHES

TRIP DETAILS

TRIP TO:

DATES FROM: / /   TO: / /

WEATHER: _____

Overall score/rating: ① ② ③ ④ ⑤ ⑥ ⑦ ⑧ ⑨ ⑩

Where we stayed:

Places we visited:

What we enjoyed most:

Favorite place(s) to eat/drink:

Places to remember next time:

NOTES & SKETCHES

TRIP DETAILS

TRIP TO:

DATES FROM: / /   TO: / /

WEATHER:

Overall score/rating: ① ② ③ ④ ⑤ ⑥ ⑦ ⑧ ⑨ ⑩

Where we stayed:

Places we visited:

What we enjoyed most:

Favorite place(s) to eat/drink:

Places to remember next time:

NOTES & SKETCHES

TRIP DETAILS

TRIP TO:

DATES FROM: / /   TO: / /

WEATHER: _____

Overall score/rating: ① ② ③ ④ ⑤ ⑥ ⑦ ⑧ ⑨ ⑩

Where we stayed:

Places we visited:

What we enjoyed most:

Favorite place(s) to eat/drink:

Places to remember next time:

NOTES & SKETCHES

TRIP DETAILS

TRIP TO:

DATES FROM: / /   TO: / /

WEATHER: ☀️ 🌤️ ☁️ 💨 🌧️ 🌨️

Overall score/rating: ① ② ③ ④ ⑤ ⑥ ⑦ ⑧ ⑨ ⑩

Where we stayed:

Places we visited:

What we enjoyed most:

Favorite place(s) to eat/drink:

Places to remember next time:

NOTES & SKETCHES

TRIP DETAILS

TRIP TO:

DATES FROM: /   /   TO: /   /

WEATHER: _____

Overall score/rating: ① ② ③ ④ ⑤ ⑥ ⑦ ⑧ ⑨ ⑩

Where we stayed:

Places we visited:

What we enjoyed most:

Favorite place(s) to eat/drink:

Places to remember next time:

NOTES & SKETCHES

TRIP DETAILS

TRIP TO:

DATES FROM: / /   TO: / /

WEATHER: ☀ ⛅ ☁ 🌬 🌧 🌨

Overall score/rating: ① ② ③ ④ ⑤ ⑥ ⑦ ⑧ ⑨ ⑩

Where we stayed:

Places we visited:

What we enjoyed most:

Favorite place(s) to eat/drink:

Places to remember next time:

NOTES & SKETCHES

TRIP DETAILS

TRIP TO:

DATES FROM: / / TO: / /

WEATHER: ☀ ⛅ ☁ 🌬 🌧 🌨

Overall score/rating: ① ② ③ ④ ⑤ ⑥ ⑦ ⑧ ⑨ ⑩

Where we stayed:

Places we visited:

What we enjoyed most:

Favorite place(s) to eat/drink:

Places to remember next time:

NOTES & SKETCHES

TRIP DETAILS

TRIP TO:

DATES FROM: / /   TO: / /

WEATHER: ☀ ⛅ ☁ 🌬 🌧 🌨

Overall score/rating: ① ② ③ ④ ⑤ ⑥ ⑦ ⑧ ⑨ ⑩

Where we stayed:
_____

Places we visited:
_____
_____
_____

What we enjoyed most:
_____
_____
_____

Favorite place(s) to eat/drink:
_____
_____
_____

Places to remember next time:
_____
_____
_____

NOTES & SKETCHES

TRIP DETAILS

TRIP TO:

DATES FROM: / /   TO: / /

WEATHER: _____

Overall score/rating: ① ② ③ ④ ⑤ ⑥ ⑦ ⑧ ⑨ ⑩

Where we stayed:

Places we visited:

What we enjoyed most:

Favorite place(s) to eat/drink:

Places to remember next time:

NOTES & SKETCHES

TRIP DETAILS

TRIP TO:

DATES FROM: / / TO: / /

WEATHER: _____ ☀️ ⛅ ☁️ 🌬️ 🌧️ 🌨️

Overall score/rating: ① ② ③ ④ ⑤ ⑥ ⑦ ⑧ ⑨ ⑩

Where we stayed:
_____

Places we visited:
_____
_____
_____
_____

What we enjoyed most:
_____
_____
_____

Favorite place(s) to eat/drink:
_____
_____
_____

Places to remember next time:
_____
_____
_____

NOTES & SKETCHES

TRIP DETAILS

TRIP TO:

DATES FROM: / /   TO: / /

WEATHER:

Overall score/rating: ① ② ③ ④ ⑤ ⑥ ⑦ ⑧ ⑨ ⑩

Where we stayed:

Places we visited:

What we enjoyed most:

Favorite place(s) to eat/drink:

Places to remember next time:

NOTES & SKETCHES

TRIP DETAILS

TRIP TO:

DATES FROM: / /   TO: / /

WEATHER:

Overall score/rating: 1 2 3 4 5 6 7 8 9 10

Where we stayed:

Places we visited:

What we enjoyed most:

Favorite place(s) to eat/drink:

Places to remember next time:

NOTES & SKETCHES

TRIP DETAILS

TRIP TO:

DATES FROM: / /   TO: / /

WEATHER: ☀ ⛅ ☁ 🌬 🌧 🌨

Overall score/rating: ① ② ③ ④ ⑤ ⑥ ⑦ ⑧ ⑨ ⑩

Where we stayed:
_____

Places we visited:
_____
_____
_____
_____

What we enjoyed most:
_____
_____
_____

Favorite place(s) to eat/drink:
_____
_____
_____

Places to remember next time:
_____
_____
_____

NOTES & SKETCHES

TRIP DETAILS

TRIP TO:

DATES FROM: / /   TO: / /

WEATHER: ☀ ⛅ ☁ 🌬 🌧 🌨

Overall score/rating: ① ② ③ ④ ⑤ ⑥ ⑦ ⑧ ⑨ ⑩

Where we stayed:

Places we visited:

What we enjoyed most:

Favorite place(s) to eat/drink:

Places to remember next time:

NOTES & SKETCHES

TRIP DETAILS

TRIP TO:

DATES FROM: / /   TO: / /

WEATHER:

Overall score/rating: ① ② ③ ④ ⑤ ⑥ ⑦ ⑧ ⑨ ⑩

Where we stayed:
_____

Places we visited:
_____
_____
_____
_____

What we enjoyed most:
_____
_____
_____

Favorite place(s) to eat/drink:
_____
_____
_____

Places to remember next time:
_____
_____
_____

NOTES & SKETCHES

TRIP DETAILS

TRIP TO:

DATES FROM: / /   TO: / /

WEATHER: _____

Overall score/rating: ① ② ③ ④ ⑤ ⑥ ⑦ ⑧ ⑨ ⑩

Where we stayed:
_____

Places we visited:
_____
_____
_____
_____

What we enjoyed most:
_____
_____
_____

Favorite place(s) to eat/drink:
_____
_____
_____

Places to remember next time:
_____
_____
_____

NOTES & SKETCHES

TRIP DETAILS

TRIP TO:

DATES FROM: / / TO: / /

WEATHER: ☀️ ⛅ ☁️ 🌬️ 🌧️ 🌨️

Overall score/rating: ① ② ③ ④ ⑤ ⑥ ⑦ ⑧ ⑨ ⑩

Where we stayed:
_____

Places we visited:
_____
_____
_____
_____

What we enjoyed most:
_____
_____
_____

Favorite place(s) to eat/drink:
_____
_____
_____

Places to remember next time:
_____
_____
_____

NOTES & SKETCHES

TRIP DETAILS

TRIP TO:

DATES FROM: / /   TO: / /

WEATHER:

Overall score/rating: ① ② ③ ④ ⑤ ⑥ ⑦ ⑧ ⑨ ⑩

Where we stayed:

Places we visited:

What we enjoyed most:

Favorite place(s) to eat/drink:

Places to remember next time:

NOTES & SKETCHES

TRIP DETAILS

TRIP TO:

DATES FROM: / /   TO: / /

WEATHER: _____

Overall score/rating: ① ② ③ ④ ⑤ ⑥ ⑦ ⑧ ⑨ ⑩

Where we stayed:
_____

Places we visited:
_____
_____
_____
_____

What we enjoyed most:
_____
_____
_____

Favorite place(s) to eat/drink:
_____
_____
_____

Places to remember next time:
_____
_____
_____

NOTES & SKETCHES

TRIP DETAILS

TRIP TO:

DATES FROM: / /   TO: / /

WEATHER:

Overall score/rating: ① ② ③ ④ ⑤ ⑥ ⑦ ⑧ ⑨ ⑩

Where we stayed:
_____

Places we visited:
_____
_____
_____
_____

What we enjoyed most:
_____
_____
_____

Favorite place(s) to eat/drink:
_____
_____
_____

Places to remember next time:
_____
_____
_____

NOTES & SKETCHES

TRIP DETAILS

TRIP TO:

DATES FROM: __ / __ / __   TO: __ / __ / __

WEATHER: ☀ ⛅ ☁ 🌬 🌧 🌨

Overall score/rating: ① ② ③ ④ ⑤ ⑥ ⑦ ⑧ ⑨ ⑩

Where we stayed:
_____
_____

Places we visited:
_____
_____
_____
_____

What we enjoyed most:
_____
_____
_____

Favorite place(s) to eat/drink:
_____
_____
_____

Places to remember next time:
_____
_____
_____

NOTES & SKETCHES

TRIP DETAILS

TRIP TO:

DATES FROM: __ / __ / __   TO: __ / __ / __

WEATHER: ☀️ ⛅ ☁️ 🌬️ 🌧️ 🌨️

Overall score/rating: ① ② ③ ④ ⑤ ⑥ ⑦ ⑧ ⑨ ⑩

Where we stayed:

Places we visited:

What we enjoyed most:

Favorite place(s) to eat/drink:

Places to remember next time:

NOTES & SKETCHES

TRIP DETAILS

TRIP TO:

DATES FROM: / /   TO: / /

WEATHER: ☀ ⛅ ☁ 🌬 🌧 🌨

Overall score/rating: ① ② ③ ④ ⑤ ⑥ ⑦ ⑧ ⑨ ⑩

Where we stayed:
_____

Places we visited:
_____
_____
_____

What we enjoyed most:
_____
_____

Favorite place(s) to eat/drink:
_____
_____
_____

Places to remember next time:
_____
_____
_____

NOTES & SKETCHES

TRIP DETAILS

TRIP TO:

DATES FROM: / /   TO: / /

WEATHER: _____

Overall score/rating: ① ② ③ ④ ⑤ ⑥ ⑦ ⑧ ⑨ ⑩

Where we stayed:
_____

Places we visited:
_____
_____
_____
_____

What we enjoyed most:
_____
_____
_____

Favorite place(s) to eat/drink:
_____
_____
_____

Places to remember next time:
_____
_____
_____

NOTES & SKETCHES

TRIP DETAILS

TRIP TO:

DATES FROM: /   /   TO: /   /

WEATHER: ☀️ 🌤️ ☁️ 🌬️ 🌧️ 🌨️

Overall score/rating: ① ② ③ ④ ⑤ ⑥ ⑦ ⑧ ⑨ ⑩

Where we stayed:
___

Places we visited:
___

What we enjoyed most:
___

Favorite place(s) to eat/drink:
___

Places to remember next time:
___

NOTES & SKETCHES

TRIP DETAILS

TRIP TO:

DATES FROM: /   /   TO: /   /

WEATHER: _____

Overall score/rating: ① ② ③ ④ ⑤ ⑥ ⑦ ⑧ ⑨ ⑩

Where we stayed:
_____

Places we visited:
_____
_____
_____
_____

What we enjoyed most:
_____
_____
_____

Favorite place(s) to eat/drink:
_____
_____
_____

Places to remember next time:
_____
_____
_____

NOTES & SKETCHES

TRIP DETAILS

TRIP TO:

DATES FROM: / /   TO: / /

WEATHER:

Overall score/rating: ① ② ③ ④ ⑤ ⑥ ⑦ ⑧ ⑨ ⑩

Where we stayed:

Places we visited:

What we enjoyed most:

Favorite place(s) to eat/drink:

Places to remember next time:

NOTES & SKETCHES

TRIP DETAILS

TRIP TO:

DATES FROM: __ / __ / __   TO: __ / __ / __

WEATHER: ☀️ ⛅ ☁️ 💨 🌧️ 🌨️

Overall score/rating: ① ② ③ ④ ⑤ ⑥ ⑦ ⑧ ⑨ ⑩

Where we stayed:
_____

Places we visited:
_____
_____
_____
_____

What we enjoyed most:
_____
_____
_____

Favorite place(s) to eat/drink:
_____
_____
_____

Places to remember next time:
_____
_____
_____

NOTES & SKETCHES

TRIP DETAILS

TRIP TO:

DATES FROM: __/__/__   TO: __/__/__

WEATHER: ☀️ ⛅ ☁️ 💨 🌧️ 🌨️

Overall score/rating: ① ② ③ ④ ⑤ ⑥ ⑦ ⑧ ⑨ ⑩

Where we stayed:
_____

Places we visited:
_____
_____
_____
_____

What we enjoyed most:
_____
_____
_____

Favorite place(s) to eat/drink:
_____
_____
_____

Places to remember next time:
_____
_____
_____

NOTES & SKETCHES

TRIP DETAILS

TRIP TO:

DATES FROM: / /   TO: / /

WEATHER:

Overall score/rating: ① ② ③ ④ ⑤ ⑥ ⑦ ⑧ ⑨ ⑩

Where we stayed:

Places we visited:

What we enjoyed most:

Favorite place(s) to eat/drink:

Places to remember next time:

NOTES & SKETCHES

TRIP DETAILS

TRIP TO:

DATES FROM: / /   TO: / /

WEATHER:

Overall score/rating: ① ② ③ ④ ⑤ ⑥ ⑦ ⑧ ⑨ ⑩

Where we stayed:

Places we visited:

What we enjoyed most:

Favorite place(s) to eat/drink:

Places to remember next time:

NOTES & SKETCHES

TRIP DETAILS

TRIP TO:

DATES FROM: __/__/__ TO: __/__/__

WEATHER: ☀️ ⛅ ☁️ 🌬️ 🌧️ 🌨️

Overall score/rating: ① ② ③ ④ ⑤ ⑥ ⑦ ⑧ ⑨ ⑩

Where we stayed:
_____

Places we visited:
_____
_____
_____
_____

What we enjoyed most:
_____
_____
_____

Favorite place(s) to eat/drink:
_____
_____
_____
_____

Places to remember next time:
_____
_____
_____

NOTES & SKETCHES

TRIP DETAILS

TRIP TO:

DATES FROM: __ / __ / __   TO: __ / __ / __

WEATHER: ☀️ ⛅ ☁️ 🌬️ 🌧️ 🌨️

Overall score/rating: ① ② ③ ④ ⑤ ⑥ ⑦ ⑧ ⑨ ⑩

Where we stayed:
_____

Places we visited:
_____
_____
_____
_____

What we enjoyed most:
_____
_____
_____

Favorite place(s) to eat/drink:
_____
_____
_____

Places to remember next time:
_____
_____
_____

NOTES & SKETCHES

TRIP DETAILS

TRIP TO:

DATES FROM: __ / __ / __   TO: __ / __ / __

WEATHER: ☀ ⛅ ☁ 🌬 🌧 🌨

Overall score/rating: ① ② ③ ④ ⑤ ⑥ ⑦ ⑧ ⑨ ⑩

Where we stayed:
_____

Places we visited:
_____
_____
_____
_____

What we enjoyed most:
_____
_____
_____

Favorite place(s) to eat/drink:
_____
_____
_____

Places to remember next time:
_____
_____
_____

NOTES & SKETCHES

TRIP DETAILS

TRIP TO:

DATES FROM: / /   TO: / /

WEATHER:

Overall score/rating: ① ② ③ ④ ⑤ ⑥ ⑦ ⑧ ⑨ ⑩

Where we stayed:
_____

Places we visited:
_____
_____
_____
_____

What we enjoyed most:
_____
_____
_____

Favorite place(s) to eat/drink:
_____
_____
_____

Places to remember next time:
_____
_____
_____

NOTES & SKETCHES

TRIP DETAILS

TRIP TO:

DATES FROM: /   /   TO: /   /

WEATHER: ☀️ ⛅ ☁️ 💨 🌧️ 🌨️

Overall score/rating: ① ② ③ ④ ⑤ ⑥ ⑦ ⑧ ⑨ ⑩

Where we stayed:

Places we visited:

What we enjoyed most:

Favorite place(s) to eat/drink:

Places to remember next time:

NOTES & SKETCHES

TRIP DETAILS

TRIP TO:

DATES FROM: __/__/__   TO: __/__/__

WEATHER:

Overall score/rating: ① ② ③ ④ ⑤ ⑥ ⑦ ⑧ ⑨ ⑩

Where we stayed:
_____

Places we visited:
_____
_____
_____

What we enjoyed most:
_____
_____
_____

Favorite place(s) to eat/drink:
_____
_____
_____

Places to remember next time:
_____
_____
_____

NOTES & SKETCHES

TRIP DETAILS

TRIP TO:

DATES   FROM: /   /   TO: /   /

WEATHER:

Overall score/rating: ① ② ③ ④ ⑤ ⑥ ⑦ ⑧ ⑨ ⑩

Where we stayed:

Places we visited:

What we enjoyed most:

Favorite place(s) to eat/drink:

Places to remember next time:

NOTES & SKETCHES

TRIP DETAILS

TRIP TO:

DATES FROM: __ / __ / __   TO: __ / __ / __

WEATHER:

Overall score/rating: ① ② ③ ④ ⑤ ⑥ ⑦ ⑧ ⑨ ⑩

Where we stayed:

Places we visited:

What we enjoyed most:

Favorite place(s) to eat/drink:

Places to remember next time:

NOTES & SKETCHES

TRIP DETAILS

TRIP TO:

DATES FROM: __ / __ / __ TO: __ / __ / __

WEATHER: _____

Overall score/rating: ① ② ③ ④ ⑤ ⑥ ⑦ ⑧ ⑨ ⑩

Where we stayed:
_____

Places we visited:
_____
_____
_____
_____

What we enjoyed most:
_____
_____
_____

Favorite place(s) to eat/drink:
_____
_____
_____

Places to remember next time:
_____
_____
_____

NOTES & SKETCHES

TRIP DETAILS

TRIP TO:

DATES FROM: /   /   TO: /   /

WEATHER:

Overall score/rating: ① ② ③ ④ ⑤ ⑥ ⑦ ⑧ ⑨ ⑩

Where we stayed:

Places we visited:

What we enjoyed most:

Favorite place(s) to eat/drink:

Places to remember next time:

NOTES & SKETCHES

TRIP DETAILS

TRIP TO:

DATES FROM: /   /   TO: /   /

WEATHER: ☀ ⛅ ☁ 💨 🌧 🌨

Overall score/rating: ① ② ③ ④ ⑤ ⑥ ⑦ ⑧ ⑨ ⑩

Where we stayed:

Places we visited:

What we enjoyed most:

Favorite place(s) to eat/drink:

Places to remember next time:

NOTES & SKETCHES

TRIP DETAILS

TRIP TO:

DATES FROM: / /   TO: / /

WEATHER:

Overall score/rating: ① ② ③ ④ ⑤ ⑥ ⑦ ⑧ ⑨ ⑩

Where we stayed:

Places we visited:

What we enjoyed most:

Favorite place(s) to eat/drink:

Places to remember next time:

NOTES & SKETCHES

TRIP DETAILS

TRIP TO:

DATES FROM: __ / __ / __   TO: __ / __ / __

WEATHER:

Overall score/rating: ① ② ③ ④ ⑤ ⑥ ⑦ ⑧ ⑨ ⑩

Where we stayed:

Places we visited:

What we enjoyed most:

Favorite place(s) to eat/drink:

Places to remember next time:

NOTES & SKETCHES

TRIP DETAILS

TRIP TO:

DATES FROM: / /   TO: / /

WEATHER:

Overall score/rating: ① ② ③ ④ ⑤ ⑥ ⑦ ⑧ ⑨ ⑩

Where we stayed:

Places we visited:

What we enjoyed most:

Favorite place(s) to eat/drink:

Places to remember next time:

NOTES & SKETCHES

TRIP DETAILS

TRIP TO:

DATES FROM: __ / __ / __   TO: __ / __ / __

WEATHER:

Overall score/rating: ① ② ③ ④ ⑤ ⑥ ⑦ ⑧ ⑨ ⑩

Where we stayed:

Places we visited:

What we enjoyed most:

Favorite place(s) to eat/drink:

Places to remember next time:

NOTES & SKETCHES

TRIP DETAILS

TRIP TO:

DATES FROM: / /   TO: / /

WEATHER:

Overall score/rating: ① ② ③ ④ ⑤ ⑥ ⑦ ⑧ ⑨ ⑩

Where we stayed:

Places we visited:

What we enjoyed most:

Favorite place(s) to eat/drink:

Places to remember next time:

NOTES & SKETCHES

TRIP DETAILS

TRIP TO:

DATES FROM: / / TO: / /

WEATHER:

Overall score/rating: ① ② ③ ④ ⑤ ⑥ ⑦ ⑧ ⑨ ⑩

Where we stayed:

Places we visited:

What we enjoyed most:

Favorite place(s) to eat/drink:

Places to remember next time:

NOTES & SKETCHES

TRIP DETAILS

TRIP TO:

DATES   FROM: /   /   TO: /   /

WEATHER: _____

Overall score/rating: ① ② ③ ④ ⑤ ⑥ ⑦ ⑧ ⑨ ⑩

Where we stayed:
_____

Places we visited:
_____
_____
_____

What we enjoyed most:
_____
_____
_____

Favorite place(s) to eat/drink:
_____
_____
_____

Places to remember next time:
_____
_____
_____

NOTES & SKETCHES

Printed in Great Britain
by Amazon